# THE
# LIFE AND TEACHINGS
# OF
# BUDDHA

# THE LIFE AND TEACHINGS OF BUDDHA

**THE ANAGARIKA DHARMAPALA**

**Buddhist Missionary, General Secretary of the Maha-Bodhi Society, Eidtor, "Maha Bodhi Journal," Special Buddhist Representative at the Chicago Parliament of Religions**

**Second Edition**

GYAN

*Published by*

Gyan Publishing House
5, Ansari Road
Daryaganj, New Delhi-110002
Phone: 011-47034999, 9811692060
E-mail: books@gyanbooks.com

*Distribution Network*
gyanbooks.com
India, USA, Canada, UK, Australia, France



ISBN : 978-81-212-2758-2 (HB)
First Published, 1918

2nd Impression 2021

*Printed at:* Gyan Press, Delhi.



**The**
**Life and Teachings of Buddha**
Author: Anagarika Dharmapala

# THE LIFE AND TEACHINGS OF BUDDHA


**THE ANAGARIKA DHARMAPALA**

*Buddhist Missionary, General Secretary of the Maha-Bodhi Society, Editor, "Maha Bodhi Journal," Special Buddhist Representative at the Chicago Parliament of Religions.*



**Second Edition.**

**PRICE As. 12.**

G. A. NATESAN & CO.

MADRAS

## CONTENTS

## *PUBLISHERS' NOTE.*

Advantage has been taken of the issue of this new edition to add a fresh chapter on "The Arya Dharma and the Coming of the Buddha of Love." We are obliged to the Anagarika Dharmapala for permission to print this important chapter from his book on "Arya Dharma" recently published by the Maha-Bodhi Society, Calcutta.

# THE LIFE AND TEACHINGS OF BUDDHA

ALTHOUGH the great Teacher of India was born in the heart of Aryavarta, yet His name is only a memory to the millions of that land. As an Avatar the Buddha is known to the readers of the Gita Govinda and the Puranas not as a redeemer, but as one who came to send people to hell by misleading them! It is inconceivable why the writers of the Puranas represented the great Lord of Compassion as one who appeared to send men to perdition. For nearly twenty-five centuries the religion of the Buddha has flourished in different parts of Asia, but in the very land where He was born, where His great religion existed till the time of the Moslem invasion, no devotees exist, except in the eastern portion of Bengal where it is accepted by a community who speak the Bengalee language. The place where the Sakyan Prince was born is in the jungles of ed thither for the destruction of the humane religion. In Turfan, Khotan, in the Yuzufsai valley, in Central Turkestan, faithful followers devoutly worshipped the Three Gems, Buddha, Dhamma, Sangha and the followers of the Brahmans had no cause to obliterate the landmarks of a religion which is ethically so similar to theirs at least in the common doctrines of Karma, Rebirth and Emancipation from suffering. Buddhism had come to India at a time, when her people were in the zenith of power, when her greatness was unquestionable. Greece was the only country then known in the West which had a civilization similar to that of India.

The gods of Greece were not hostile to the Aryan gods of India and the customs and manners of ancient Greece were not so absolutely opposed to the Aryan customs of pre-Christian India. No Western conqueror dared to invade India since the defeat of the cohorts of the great Alexander, who perished soon after his retreat in Babylon in his thirtieth year. Western countries of the Mediterranean slope knew India as a country of wealth and great learning. The Greek ambassadors who had sojourned in Middle India in the Court of Chandragupta and his great successors had recorded the strength and power of the people of India. They were a great and noble people who never violated their word once given, and Megasthenes knew their moral capabilities. Neither the Persians, nor the Greeks, nor the Romans were hostile to the Indian people. Themselves civilized and appreciating the gifts of a settled civilization they were contented to trade with the people of India and Ceylon. Roman ambassadors visited the courts of the Indian and Ceylonese kings, and ambassadors of India and Ceylon were sent to the Imperial Court of Rome. The Romans learnt the secrets of imperialism from India. The gorgeous processions, majestic durbars, presided by kings who claimed relationship with the illuminating Sun, who reigned from sea to sea with the title of "Raja Chakravarti," whose armies consisted of 200,000 horses, 10,000 elephants, a million of infantry, whose sway extended above and below for a mile, struck awe in the minds of ambassadors who visited the camps of the Indian Emperors. India was free from invasion for one thousand years, the very period when she was supreme and when the Dharma of the Buddha dominated the land far and wide. If morality had achieved victories it was during this memorable period, five hundred years before and five hundred years after the so-called Christian era. Where is the empire that had stood for a millennium of years before or after, since the downfall of Buddhism in India ? Buddha's teachings at this period spread all over the civilized portions of Asia and made the people happy. Where they were still barbarous the gentle Doctrine of Love and Brotherhood modified their beliefs and customs.

Antiquarians and archæologists have come to our rescue pointing out the marvellous structures which were built by the Buddhists when they were yet alive, before they were annihilated by the barbarians who cared for neither man nor celestial being, whose one object was plunder and the satisfaction of their unbridled lust. From the barren plains of Arabia came the torch that was to set fire to many an ancient civilization, and the heartless Vandals began their mad career of destruction annihilating everything that came before them. We are concerned only with the civilization of Aryan India and the ramifications which had extended as far as Bamian, Central Asia, Turfan, Afghanistan, Candahar, Khotan, Kashmir, developed by the potency of the Dharma of the Tathagato. The wonderful remains now being discovered by the indefatigable labours of Oriental scholars like Stein, Pischel, Grunwedel, and Le Coq in Chinese Turkestan are splendid evidence showing the vastness of the influence of the Buddha's Empire. Unlearned critics not knowing the conditions that had existed outside India in the eighth century naturally came to the conclusion that Buddhism had met its fate at the hands of such men like Kumarila Bhatta and Sankara. They had no idea of the ruins wherein were buried evidences to show that in the eleventh century of the European era Buddhism was yet alive in the Magadha Kingdom ; and the copper-plate grants discovered at Sahet Mahet show that the famous temple at Sravasti was still under the occupation of the Buddhists at the time of Govinda Chandra. Sankara and Kumarila Bhatta may have waged polemical wars with Buddhist monks, but to prove that they were instrumental in the obliteration of Buddhism from its birthplace sufficient evidence of an antiquarian nature is not forthcoming. In the eleventh century Buddhism found its dread foe in Bhaktiar Khilji, the great Vandal who destroyed the libraries of Nalanda and Odantapuri. The Buddhism of the people of India was of native origin, the gods of the Buddhist were the gods of the Brahman. Throughout the long reign of Buddhist kings the Brahman and the Sramanas were the objects of devout charity. The chief disciples of the Tathagato were high class Brahmans, the Presidents of the great Convocations were Brahman Bhikkhus, and Buddhist kings had Brahman purohits to officiate at their Coronations. Even to-day in Siam where a Buddhist king reigns, the ceremonies at the

Coronation are celebrated according to Brahmanical rites, and Brahman priests officiate. So far history is silent as to a war between Buddhists and Brahmans. Politically there were wars between kings of Buddhist and Brahman countries, but of persecutions to annihilate each other we find no signs in contemporary history. Ceylon had always remained a Buddhist kingdom, and in the twelfth century there was a great revival of Buddhism under the great king Parakrama Bahu, and in his Court were a thousand Brahmans; and to-day at Polonnaruwa ruins of ancient temples and Brahmanical devalayas are being explored, and sculptures both Buddhist and Brahman are being discovered showing that one common enemy had wrought havoc on both. In Buddha Gaya and Sarnath in Benares images of the Hindu gods have been found mutilated along with the statues of the Buddha and the Bodhisatwas. In Ceylon to-day the Buddhists have built the images of Brahmanical gods in their temples. The Buddhist kings were great upholders of Brahmanical ceremony, and they were also supporters of the Bhikkhus and upheld the Religion of the Lord Buddha. The griha dharma of the Buddhists were identical with those of the Brahmans, the ten evils to abstain from are the common property of both the Brahmans and the Buddhists, the names of the hells of both the religions are identical, so also the heavens and the presiding deities; and the only point on which only the highly philosophical student would venture to argue, is the doctrine of Anatta. The great gulf that divided the two great families in India began after the invasion of India by Mahmud of Ghazni. Since that event the gulf became wider because every successor to the throne of the iconoclast was bound to continue the work of destruction. In India the Persian word Buthparas meant at first a Buddhist but later on an image worshipper. Its origin may be traced to the early times before the invading Persian came to India. The iconoclasts knew Buth before they came to India, in Bamian, in Turfan, in Khotan. And in India they found "Buth" in every great temple wherever they had penetrated.

And as there had been no effort to know what Buddhism was under the Moslem sway, the great Teacher's memory lived only as an Avatar, the god who came in the form of Mercy. The ninth Avatara of the Puranas is no doubt intended for the Compassionate one. As for the other charge that Buddha was against the Vedas, it is only used as an argument by the Brahmans, but in the suttas of the Pali pitakas nowhere do we find one word against the Vedas. What we do find is that at first there had been no institution of sacrifices of animals, and that the animal sacrifices were first organised by the Brahmans during the reign of king Ikhsvaku. Thus do we find in the Brahmanadhammika sutta of the Sutta Nipata :—

So it was heard by me :

At one time the Blessed One dwelt at Savatthi in Jetavana in the monastery of Anathapindika. Then many wealthy Brahmans of Kosala, advanced in age, went to the Blessed One and after having exchanged greetings with Him asked " O excellent Gotama, are the Brahmans now-a-days seen engaged in the Brahmanical customs of old? And the Blessed One answered, "The Brahmans now-a-days are not seen engaged in the Brahman customs of ancient days" and the Brahmans thereupon said, "May the excellent Gotama tell us of the ancient customs of the Brahmans of old," and the Blessed One answered :—

"The ancient rishis were well restrained, penitent, and they controlled their senses, and they studied their own welfare. There were no cattle for the Brahmans, nor gold, nor corn, and their wealth was meditation, and they kept watch over this treasure. Inviolable were the Brahmans, protected by the Dharma, and for forty-eight years they practised the holy Bramachariya life, and they were of exemplary conduct. The Brahmans did not marry women belonging to another caste, nor did they buy a wife; they chose living together in mutual love after having come together. He who was the best of the Brahmans did not even in sleep dream of sexual pleasure. Imitating his practices some wise men in this world praised chastity, virtue and patience. Having asked for rice, beds, garments, butter, and oil, they made sacrifices out of them, and when sacrifice came on they did not kill cows. Cows are our best friends, they are like unto a mother, father, brother, and other relatives. The cows give us nourishment and they give us milk—and the Brahmans did not kill cows. So long as they did not kill cows the race prospered. Later on a change came, and the Brahmans became covetous, seeking wealth and beautiful women. They composed hymns and went to king Ikhsvaku and said " Thou hast much wealth and corn, and thou must make sacrifice," and the king, lord of chariots, instructed by the Brahmans brought about the sacrifices of Aswamedha, Purisamedha, Sammapasa, Vacapeyya. And the Brahmans caused the sacrifice of many hundred thousand cows. Then the gods, the pitris, Indra, the Asuras and the Rakshasas cried out "this is injustice," for the cows have been slain. The Brahmans of old fell from their high state, discord arose, and the Brahmans and the Kshatriyas fell into the power of sensual pleasure."

We assert that the author of the Bhagavad-Gita was more hostile to the Vedas than the author of the Suttas in the Pali Pitakas, for nowhere do we find such a strong denunciation of the Vedas as the following:—

**Yávánartha udapáne sarvatah samplutodake**
**Távánsarveshu vedeshu bráhmanasyavijánatah**

All the Vedas are as useful to an enlightened Brahmana as is a tank in a place covered all over with water.

[Bhagavad Gita, II. 46.]

The Buddhism of the Pali Pitakas came to be recognised with the decipherment of the Asoka inscriptions. For when Princep came across the Magadhi name of "Devanam piya piyadasina" there was not one Brahman scholar in all India who could guess even the meaning, and it was left to the Ceylon Bhikkhus to elucidate the word which they did by referring to the Mahavansa, through Turnour, who, at the time, was a Government official in Ceylon and was in communication with the Bhikkhus of the Kandy Temple. The word was identified and henceforth Pali was found to be a necessity in the elucidation of ancient Indian history. This was in 1837. Then forty years later Childers began his labours in the field of Pali, and to him we owe the beginning of Pali development. Then came the great scholar and indefatigable worker, now known all over the world—Professor T. W. Rhys Davids—for his beautiful translations of Pali suttas along with Fausboll, Trenkner, Morris, and others, and now we know what the Blessed One had taught to the people of ancient India when she was in the zenith of her glory.

## BIRTH OF THE FUTURE BUDDHA

In the Kaliyuga year 2478 on the full moon day of Vaisakha, in the royal grove of Lumbini, midway between Devadaha and Kapilavastu the future Buddha was born. His mother was the saintly Maya, wife of king Suddhodana. They belonged to the Kshattriyas of the Gautama gotra, of the Sakya clan of the solar race, tracing their descent from the family of King Ikhsvaku. Since that date 2541 years have elapsed and many great empires have declined and many new empires have come and gone, and several new world religions have appeared which to-day dominate the world—Christianity, Islam, Vaishnavism and Sikhism. The only religion which appeals to all enlightened men of all castes and creeds is the Religion of Dharma promulgated by the Buddha Gautama Sakya Muni, about whom Sir Edwin Arnold in his exquisitely beautiful poem, the "Light of Asia" sang :—

> . ...Saviour of the World,
> Lord Buddha—Prince Siddhartha styled on earth—
> In Earth and Heavens and Hells Incomparable,
> All-honored, Wisest, Best, most Pitiful;
> The Teacher of Nirvana and the Law.

On the day that the future Buddha was conceived, it is said that an immeasurable light spread throughout the ten thousand worlds, the blind recovered their sight, the deaf received their hearing, the dumb talked, the lame walked, fires went out in all the hells, diseased men became well, wild animals timid, all mortals became gentle of speech, a mild, cool breeze began to blow, &c. And on the day that the future Buddha was born the babe divine was first received by the god Brahma, and He was placed before His mother saying " Rejoice O Queen! A mighty son has been born to thee," and all the gods spake saying ' Great Being there is none your equal, much less your superior,' and the Babe performed a miracle by the phenomenal uttering, " the chief am I in all the world. " And on the day that the future Buddha was born there was born also the Princess Yasodhara, his future wife, and also the Bo-tree that was to give him shade on the day that He was to become supremely Enlightened, and also his courtier as well as his horse.

The Raja Suddhodana was delighted that so great a son has been born to him, and he invited Brahmans to his palace and gave them delicious food in golden bowls and presents of the most costly cloth. It so happened that the Rishi Kaladeva, teacher of the Raja Suddhodana, having heard of the celestial rejoicings in Indra's heaven inquired the cause and he was told that a son was born to the Raja Suddhodana who would become Buddha, the teacher of gods and men, and the Rishi thereupon miraculously transported himself and descended in the palace grounds of the Raja, and the King thereat rejoiced that his teacher had come to bless the child. With great ceremony the child was presented by the royal father to the Rishi to be blessed; but instead the Rishi arose from his seat saying:—

> O babe, I worship! Thou art He!
> I see the rosy light, the foot sole marks,
> The soft curled tendril of the Swastika,
> The sacred primal signs thirty and two,
> The Eighty lesser tokens. Thou art Buddha,
> And thou wilt preach the Law and save all flesh
> Who learn the Law, though I shall never hear,
> Dying too soon, who lately longed to die;
> Howbeit I have seen Thee. Know O King!
> This is that Blossom on our human tree
> Which opens once in many myriad years—
> But opened, fills the world with Wisdom's scent
> And Love's dropped honey; from thy royal root
> A heavenly Lotus springs: Ah happy House!

The Brahman astrologers prophesied that the Prince, who was named Siddhartha, would grow up to manhood and that if he remained in the family he would become a supreme King-Emperor, a Chakravarti; if he renounced the worldly life, then he would become the World Teacher, the Buddha Supreme. On the seventh day of the Prince's birth, his mother died and was born in the Tusita heaven, for no more was she to bear the sufferings of the human world. A future Buddha till the attainment of the supreme state of *Anuttara Samma Sambodhi* is known as the Bodhisat; and it is a *dharmata* of the Buddha ideal that in the last birth of the Bodhisat, his mother can only survive for seven days after the birth of the divine Child, for on the eighth day she expires to be born in heaven.

THE BOYHOOD OF THE FUTURE BUDDHA

The King delighted at the joyful news ordered that three palaces should be erected for the three Indian seasons, one for the summer, another for the rainy season, and the other for the winter. In the Anguttara Nikaya, 3rd Nipata, the description of the three palaces is given, and also the methods adopted by the king to teach the divine boy, and the amusements provided for him in the way of water sports, boating, archery, riding, &c. Thus the holy Child grew amid the joyous surroundings of the Sakyan capital of Kapilavastu on the Himalayan slope. The full details of the Bodhisat's youthful life may be found in the Jataka translated by Rhys Davids. (Trubner's

Series). In the sixteenth year the Prince was married to his cousin the Princess Bimba, more familiarly known as Yasodhara, mother of the Prince Rahula. She was of the same age as the Prince Siddhartha, and the Books declare that for countless millions of years, life after life, she was the wife of the future Buddha, for she had made the vow that she would take the Bodhisat as her husband, and that she would hear the Law and enter Nirvana. And the Jatakas give us many many birth stories showing the devout attachment which she as his consort had for him throughout the Bodhisat career. The touching pathos of her devotion is admirably depicted in the life story when the Bodhisat was born as the Prince Vessantara with whom and with her two children she goes to the forest to observe the ascetic life. The Prince adopted the life of a rajarishi, and when living the holy life a Brahman came and asked the Prince to give him his two children. Now the *dharmata* of a Bodhisattva is that whatever is asked for, and by whomsoever the request is made, the gift is given with a prarthana that by the force of that karma may the Buddhahood be reached. And when the Brahman demanded that the two children be given to him, the Prince willingly gave them, and at the time the gift was made, the Princess Madri had gone to fetch fruits, and on her return she found that the children were missing, and seeing the silence of the Prince began to lament for the loss, and weeping fell down at his feet in a swoon. The Prince showing his tender love and helping her to recover consciousness, had to confess that in her absence the children were offered to a Brahman, because the man came and demanded that the children should be given to him, and a refusal was impossible, but that they were offered to him with the aim of reaching the supreme position of Buddhahood and to save all life, and that she should also show her concurrence with the gift and not obstruct the great consummation. She willingly assented and both rejoiced that with the sacrifice they had made they had shown the highest love for the salvation of the world, for in a later book we read "that greater love hath no man that he gave his only begotten son for the salvation of the world." Not in one life, but in a thousand lives, did the future Buddha with a willing heart, in the fulfilment of Paramitas often give his most cherished possessions, and his blood, his limbs, his eyes, &c., for the acquirement of the absolute Wisdom of the Bodhi for the salvation of the world, of beings born during a kalpa. So great was his love for all life born and unborn, and it is this love absolute shown by the Bodhisat that has endeared His memory for countless millions of human beings these twenty-five hundred years. In the fulfilment of the ten perfections the Bodhisat is supreme, and no hero has been the recipient of so much love in return from so large a portion of humanity in the continent of Asia. The missionary spirit of the ancient Bhikkhus of India was made manifest six months after the Prince Siddhartha reached the supreme Buddhahood at Buddha Gaya, under the shade of the great Bodhi Tree, whereat He sat on the full moon day of Vesakha 2500 years ago.

## THE INITIATION OF THE BODHISAT

The supreme perfections which a Bodhisatva is expected to fulfil, not for one life but for countless lives, for a period of four asankhya kalpas, are Dana, Sila, Naishkramya, Pragna, Virya, Satya, Kshanti, Adhisthana, Maitri and Upeksha.

Dana is to give; and in the giving of wealth, limbs, life, and children for the good of humanity consists the supreme dana.

Sila is the virtuous life of moral purity, refraining from giving pain to any living being.

Naishkramya is the life of renunciation, sacrificing self for the good of humanity.

Pragna is supreme Wisdom where Error findeth no place.

Virya is strenuous endeavour, persevering exertion till the consummation is reached, by avoiding evil, and generating the good.

Satya is truthfulness even at the risk of life inasmuch as "truthfulness is immortal speech and this is an old rule."

Kshanti is unruffled patience and sweet

forgiveness even when one is put to torture by one's enemy.

Adhisthana is the development of the resolute, undaunted will that conquers all opposition giving power to realize one's cherished desires for the welfare of humanity and of all life.

Maitri is all-embracing love that is manifest in the mother love, which is shown to all, near and far, visible and invisible, small and great.

Upeksha is equanimity, showing no ill-will even to one's persecutor.

These are the Paramitas which must be fulfilled by every one who wishes to reach the goal of Wisdom and Love embodied in the perfect life of the Arhatas, Pratyeka Buddhas and Sammasambuddhas.

The Bodhisat who became the Buddha as Sakya Muni began his Buddha career four asankheyyas and one hundred thousand kalpas ago under the Buddha Dipamkara when he was born in a Brahman family and was leading the life of a Brahmarishi. The resolution that he then made under that

Buddha was made unquenchable and life after life he persevered, receiving the initiation at the hands of succeeding Buddhas from Dipamkara to the Buddha Kasyapa, in all twenty-four. In the Jataka Commentary the potency of the resolution is thus given: "The man who, if all within the rim of the world were to become water, would be ready to swim across it with his own arms and get to the further shore,—he is the one to attain the Buddhaship; or in case all within the rim of the world were to become live coals, would be ready to tread on them and so get to the further side,—he is the one to attain the Buddhaship;" etc.

### THE GREAT RENUNCIATION

In the twenty-ninth year of their age the Prince Siddhartha and Princess Yasodhara were blessed with a son, and on the day that the son was born, the Prince made the Great Renunciation. The Raja Suddhodana knowing that the Prince would retire from the world as the soothsayers had predicted, kept him within the palace grounds with guards placed at different stations to prevent *old* men, diseased men, &c., from entering the palace grounds, lest the Prince seeing these evil omens might get disgusted of the householder's life, but on the day that the joyous event was to occur—the birth of the child to Prince Siddhartha—the King gave permission for his going out to see the city. The chariots were ordered and the Prince proceeded on to the park enjoying the beautiful sights, and receiving the homage of his people. It was on this occasion that the gods took counsel to show him the four sights, and one of them took the shape of a decrepit old man leaning on a staff and showed himself to the future Buddha, and it is said that the sight was visible only to the Prince and the charioteer, and the Prince asked the charioteer "Who was this man leaning on a staff," and the charioteer answered: "Prince, this man was once young and strong but with age he has lost his youth and now he is old," and the Prince seeing this figure began to reflect, and proceeding further he saw a diseased man, and on inquiry, he was told that all men born must some day get ill, and the Prince reflecting was proceeding on, when he met a dead body, and on inquiry found that it was the condition to which all men should arrive, and the Prince thoughtfully was proceeding when he met the figure of a Bhikshu dressed in yellow garment with a serene countenance sitting under the foot of a shady tree, and this gave the Prince immense delight and asked the charioteer about the life of the Bhikshu, and he was told that this monk, seeing the sufferings of the world and disgusted with the sensualities of life, had renounced all and had taken to this life of solitude. The Prince delighted, then and there resolved that that very night he would make the renunciation, and returning to his palace, in the middle of the night he ordered his charioteer to bring his faithful steed and mounting his horse with his charioteer left the city. He went as far as the frontiers of his kingdom, and gave order to the charioteer to lead back the horse to the city and to give the royal robes to his father. Standing on the bank of the river Anoma, he cut off his hair and with the jewelled chaplet he threw it up declaring that it was his will that if he was to be the Buddha the hair will remain in the sky, and so it happened: the hair remained fixed in the sky, and the Ajanta sculptures show that the Indra came down and had the sacred hair removed to his celestial mansion for him to pay homage. The child that was born was given the name of Rahula and he was lovingly brought up by the Raja Suddhodana.

## THE ASCETIC LIFE

Wearing the yellow garment of a Bhikshu the Bodhisat Prince walked on foot to the capital city of the King Bimbisara of Magadha. The people of Rajagriha seeing the majestic mien of the golden complexioned ascetic did not know who he was. Some thought that it was a celestial being come down on earth, some thought that it was a naga in the shape of man come to their city, and the royal spies went and told the king that a human being of unsurpassing beauty had appeared in the city and that they did not know who he was, and the king thereupon ordered his men to watch him and bring him word, and the messengers then found that he proceeded to the Pandava Rock and there he sat and partook of his food, which he had got by begging from the people. The Prince never before having eaten anything except that which was specially prepared by the royal cooks, was, seeing this hotchpotch, disgusted, and thought of throwing it away, but His reflections on the impermanency of things and that he had left all pleasures for the sake of removing the sufferings of the world, gave him strength to eat the disgusting food. The royal messengers seeing the Prince went to the King and said that he was a human being and that he was then living at the Pandava Rock, and the King Bimbisara came to the place in royal state and asked the Prince whence he had come and what was his mission; and the Prince said that he was a Kshatriya of the Adityavamsa and that his kingdom was on the Himalayan slope, and that he had renounced the world to seek the Nirvana, being disgusted with the pleasures of the senses. The King then found out that the Prince was the son of his friend, and that he was five years younger than the Bodhisatva; and he therefore asked him to stay in his kingdom, and offered that they would jointly rule the kingdom; but to this proposal the Bodhisatva did not agree, and then he left Rajagriha and came to the sylvan wood of Uruvela, noted as a place suited for ascetics, and on the bank of the river Neranjara he began to exert himself for the consummation of his cherished desires. In the Sutta Nipata Padhana sutta, the Prince expresses himself that he will not swerve from the path even if his flesh and blood dry up, and "that it is better to die in the field of battle than to live a defeated life." Such resoluteness is only possible for one who has made the great Renunciation, and with that Kshatriya determination he began to mortify his body, for it was the philosophy of the day that Truth was obtainable through asceticism, and for six years the Bodhisat went through the severest forms of ascetic penances till he found that no more was possible for a human being to proceed; and one day his strength failed and he fell down in a swoon. In the Bhaybherava sutta the terrific penances which he had undergone for six years are categorically given, and at last when he found that asceticism was of no avail, he began to take food moderately and then he began to make the effort according to the middle path. He found that that is the only Path which brought Him illumination, and on the full moon day of the month of Vesakha He attained the supreme state of Buddha, the fully enlightened One, the Holy Arhant Buddha, the Teacher of gods and men.

## THE CHARACTERISTICS OF THE BUDDHA

To know the life of Buddha in its completeness it is necessary to go through the whole of the three Pitakas, for from the day of His Enlightenment to the day of His anupadisesa parinibbana, the strenuous life of the Great Teacher is revealed in each of the Suttas. To know the Buddha it is necessary to know the Dharma, and in the Dharma the Buddha is identified. The Buddha ordered Vakkali, the devout disciple who wished to be near Him gazing at His glorified body, to go away from his presence, with the remark that this loathsome body should not be made an object of sensual love; and Vakkali in sorrow left the Blessed One, and went to Kalasila Rock and wished to commit suicide, when the Buddha like a flash of lightning, appeared before him and dissuaded him, declaring that to know the Buddha one must know the Dharma, and when the Dharma is known the Buddha is seen. For seven weeks the Blessed One consciously enjoying the bliss of Nirvana remained at and near Buddha Gaya, and then travelled on foot to Isipatana, Migadawa, in search of the five Brahman ascetics, Kondanya, Bhaddiya, Vappa, Mahanama and Assaji who had remained with the Blessed One at Uruvela when He was going through the ascetic experiences, and who had left Him when they found that he was treading the Middle Path. In ancient Indian philosophy the highest form of religion consisted in mortifying the body. Two religions were known to the people of ancient India, the religion of the gods, and the religion of the ascetic. The householders were under the control of a hierarchy of priests who officiated and propitiated the gods. They were the mediators between gods and men, and sacrifices, rituals, ceremonies, baptisms, etc., were formulated by the priests with an eye to material gain. Animal sacrifices and oblations were the order of the day, and the priests were always on the look out for the sacrifices, inhaling the fragrance that was wafted along the zephyrs of oblations. In the Balapandita sutta of the Majjhima Nikaya is given an account of the oblation-loving Brahman in quest of ahuti-gandha. Sensualism in its most extravagant form had its votaries and the Buddha began His triumphant conquest in a land where the two extremes of religion met. The Tathagato, the successor of the former Buddhas, began His Message at the Deer Park, now Sarnath, in Benares, promulgating the Middle Doctrine of the Noble Eightfold Path, the law that doth illumine the mind and bringeth happiness in this life, in perfect consciousness. Great Brahmans became His disciples and wearing the yellow robe they went from place to place, from town to town, from country to country preaching that the Buddha has appeared and that the Dharma is being preached, and that the kulaputras have renounced the sensual life to lead the perfect life of the Brahmachari. Kings from their thrones came down to listen to the holy Gospel of Love and Compassion and of Holiness.

It was like the reception of a monarch by his loving subjects that the people of India, full of virility, knowing nothing of subjugation, welcomed the Gospel of all-embracing Love and Wisdom. Absolute emancipation in this life, on earth, in perfect consciousness,—such a Doctrine never heard of before, was promised by one who had Himself realized it. He who had made the great Renunciation, the son of the Sakya family, in the prime of life, as a youth, roaring the lion's roar of triumphant victory over Death, old age, who was there to defeat Him? It was an easy conquest, and the great Doctrine spread and expanded and within the period of forty-five years, the Blessed One had realized Himself that the Doctrine that He had preached could now be continued by His disciples, and in the eightieth year of His age the Bhavagan, Arahat Samma Sambuddha, Sakya Muni, the Tathagata, preaching the Doctrine of Immortal Activity, Self-reliance and Freedom, laid on His right side on the prepared bed between two sala trees at the Malliyan Grove, at Kusinara, and having entered into the fourth stage of Dhyanic undifferentiated illumination, passed away into the Anupadi sesa parinibbana, where neither men nor gods could see. The last disciple that the Blessed One converted was the Brahman Paribbajaka Subhadra, and the last words that the Blessed One uttered have still a meaning and till the end of time shall not cease to reverberate, for they inculcate the Supreme lesson of immortalising activity and unceasing change. "Handa dani Bhikkhave amantayami vo vaya dhamma Samkhara, appamadena sampadethati." Ayam tathagatassa pacchima vaca.

## THE PHILOSOPHY OF THE BUDDHA

The first discovery that the Buddha made is of absolute importance for the welfare of the whole world. He promulgated what had not been proclaimed before Him by either god or man. It was no haphazard stray utterance, but one of stupendous significance to those who are in search of the goal of absolute Freedom from all sankharas. That is what the Buddha discovered, and this secret he triumphantly proclaimed to the Aryan Kulaputras of noble family who were willing to realize the great Truth by leading the supreme life of Brahmachariyam.

There is pain, misery, lamentation, despair, sorrow, grief, decay, disease, dissolution and disintegration in this phenomenal world and who is there to deny it? Now what the Blessed One discovered was the cause and the cessation thereof. It is this that inquiring minds will always seek; and the Doctrine that He set before His mind's eye for later elucidation to the world is known as the Paticca samuppada, Dependent Causation, which begins with the formula "that being thus, this comes to be; from the coming to be of that this arises. That being not so this disappears. From the cessation of that, this ceases." Rhys Davids in the Introduction to the Maha Nidana Sutta, "Dialogues of Buddha," Part II, Vol. III, of the series known as "Sacred Books of the Buddhists," says, "It was not the fact of Dukkha, nor the fairly obvious conditions of birth and so on, leading up to it, that come as a revelation to each Buddha, beneath his Bo-tree. It was the process of Samudaya and Nirodha as a natural and universal law. Coming to pass! coming to pass! At that thought there arose in me a vision into things not called before to mind, and knowledge arose, insight, wisdom, light arose. Not uncaused and casually, nor by the fiat of Isvara, Indra, Soma, Varuna, Brahma—did events happen, painful or otherwise; not as Job and the Psalmist taught—'God distributeth sorrows in his anger.' For God is a righteous judge, and God is angry every day. Job XXI, 17; Psalms VII. 2. Events came impelled by preceding conditions, causes that man could by intelligence and good will, study and govern, suspend or intensify.

"Let it be remembered that the 'immanent'

absolution opposed by Buddhism was chiefly Brahmanic theosophy. According to this, the atman of the individual was not so much an efflux of the World-Atman, as was the latter immanent in, and identified with, each man-soul. 'In the beginning this world was only Soul, in the shape of a man . . . World-guardian, World-lord, this that is My Soul. 'My Soul' was therefore, in that theosophy, the personal First cause and Final cause. And hence the Paticca Samuppada of Buddhism was as decided a negation of all teleology as was the theorem of Demokritus and his master Leukippus, that 'nothing happens by chance, but everything through a cause and necessity'.

"Had the fates been kinder to the writings of the Atomist of Abdera, had the 'teleological reaction' not been led by two men of such extraordinary genius as Plato and Aristotle, it is conceivable that the whole philosophy, not to say the Dharma, of the West, might have flowed along a channel in which the influence of *mikros* and the *megas Diakosmos* might have brought both that philosophy and that Dharma more nearly parallel to the informing principle of the Paticca samuppada. As it happened, Europe, learned to believe in a universe governed partly by necessity and partly by chance, learned to combine belief in unchanging natural law with belief in first and final causes.

"And so gradually has the realm of regular, causal sequence encroached upon that of the casual and the arbitrary, that on no period in the intellectual development of Europe can we place our finger and say:— Here the concept of a universe governed, as to its every movement and happening, by natural causation, was brought home to the minds of men—to the mind of one man. There is nothing resembling the intellectual earthquake caused half a century ago by that extension of the law of Causation: the theory of Evolution.

"In the history of Indian thought, on the other hand, we can point to such an epoch-making crisis, we can discern the significance of the law of universal causation breaking in on a great mind with a flash of intuition. The law, we read, stands as fundamental, whether Tathagatas have arisen or not. But the Tathagata penetrates and masters it, and delivers the knowledge thereof to the world.'*

## II.

It is said that in the fourth week after the Buddhahood, the Blessed One enunciated the Basic Laws of Universal Causality whose complex operations are worked out in twenty-four categories under the subject of Paccayas in the book of Patthana of the Abhidhamma Pitaka. It is in the Patthana that the Laws are explained in their extremely marvellous complexity indicating the wonderful nature of the operating causes. It is here that the supreme majesty of the Wisdom's Law is shown in all its fulness, it is in the Patthana that the supreme Wisdom of the Tathagata is brought into vivid objectivity. It is only the select that can get even a glimpse of the stupendous volume of glory that belongs to the Buddha domain. Just as the *timira pingala* leviathans of the great ocean love to sport in the unfathomable waters thereof, so it is said that the Blessed One found in the deep waters of the Law of Universal Causality absolute scope for the exhibition of the immeasurable Wisdom of anavarananana which is the exclusive property of the sammasam-Buddha, the supreme Chief of the three realms of Akasa, Satta, and Sankhara. The more the Blessed One dived into the depths the more there was found room for the expression of His supreme knowledge, and in the unbounded delight that He experienced in having found the solution of the problem, there went forth from His transfigured body luminous rays of exquisite colour. From His head and eyes, lips and body, and hands and feet variegated colours of nila, pita, lohita, odata, manjesta, pabhassara emanated forming a body of glory. Rays of blue emanated from His head and eyes, golden-yellow from His body, crimson from His lips, lustrous-white from His pearl-white teeth, scarlet from the palms of His hand and the soles of His feet, the whole forming into a blending of majestic radiance issuing forth as if they were flaming messengers running before Him announcing His visit to His devout followers. On great occasions by His will-power the Blessed One intensifies the luminosity of the Buddharasmi forming into garlands radiating the sky and illuminating dark places. The rationale of the Buddharasmi is given in the Abbhutacchariya sutta of the Majjhima Nikaya, and the generating causes are enumerated in the Lakkhana sutta of the Digha nikaya. The science of the mahapurisalakkhana symbols of the great man is enunciated in the Mahapadana sutta of the Digha nikaya. It was a science known to the Brahman astrologers of ancient India, and the two beings that are heirs to the lakkhanas are the Raja Cakkavatti and the Araham Sammasam Buddha—the Emperor of a continent and the Buddha fully enlightened. The difference in the two being found in the solitary urna between the eyebrows which is like unto a tilaka spot.

The hallowed site where the Prince Bodhisatva gained the omniscient knowledge is sacred to the countless millions of Buddhists that have lived and shall live for five thousand years from the date of the Buddhahood. The consecrated spots at Buddha Gaya are the Great Tree under whose shade the supreme knowledge dawned, the spot whereon He remained gazing at the Tree in homage of the supreme Wisdom that made Him supreme above all gods and men in the three worlds, the Cloister wherein He walked contemplating the Nidanas twelve, the spot where He meditated on the Universal law of Causality, the spot where He received the two merchants, the spot where he sat during the seven days, rain protected by the Naga king, and the spot where He decided to preach the Dhamma to the World.

When seven weeks had elapsed the Blessed One went in search of the five Brahman ascetics who had been his help-mates when He was undergoing the severe ascetic penances at Uruvela, and who had left Him when they found that He had given up the extreme practices of Hathayoga. In accordance with the old established laws of asceticism as enunciated in the Hathayoga science the Bodhisat practised every kind of mortification for six years, and the experience He gained thereby showed Him the absolute futility of physical torture to gain knowledge, and when his body had reached a stage that resulted in his falling down in a swoon for want of vitality, and after He had recovered his consciousness, He decided that asceticism was not going to help Him to get knowledge and happiness. And He began to take food in moderate quantity, and the ascetic friends seeing Him eating food, lost faith in Him, and reflecting that where he had failed by his asceticism, it was useless to expect that he will gain omniscience in living the life of plenty, they abandoned Him. To eat one meal a day according to them was living a life of ease and plenty, and they departed and came to the famous spot at Benares now known as Sarnath, then Isipatana, the Deer Park. The Blessed One starting from the Bodhi met on the way between Bodhi and Gaya a naked ascetic, who questioned the Buddha "Who art thou friend?" And the Buddha answered :

All-conquering have I now become,
All-knowing, untainted by the elements of being,
Renounced have I all things, and free from all cravings,
Mine is all Wisdom, no teacher have I.
My equal nowhere can be found,
In all the worlds of gods and men
There is none to rival me,
Supreme holiness have I gained,
The teacher am I unsurpassed,
I am the Buddha supreme,
Lust's fire is quenched, Nibbana gained.
To proclaim the doctrine I seek
The city by name Kasi,
And for this blinded world I'll cause
The drum of Immortality to beat.

Then Upaka, the ascetic, said, you claim to be the immeasurable Conqueror, and the Blessed One said, "Verily it is so, I have conquered and am a Conqueror." And the Blessed One proceeded on foot to Benares, to the place where the five Bhikkhus were staying. And when they saw the Blessed One they agreed among themselves that they would not salute him, nor rise and go to meet him, and yet when He approached them, they felt the gracious majesty that made them unconsciously rise and serve him. A mat was given, and water to wash the feet, and they addressed the Blessed One by name and as their equal, and the Blessed One addressing them said, "Address not the Tathagato by name for he is the supreme Buddha. Listen, Immortality has been won, and the Doctrine will be taught to you." But the five Bhikkhus said, "Brother Gotama, those practices of yours, that method of procedure, those stern austerities did not enable you to transcend human limitations and attain to pre-eminence in sublime knowledge. How, then, now that you are luxurious, can you have transcended human limitations?" "O Bhikkhus, the Tathagato is not luxurious; the immortal path has been found; if ye will do according to my instructions, in no long time, and in the present life, ye shall learn for yourselves, and shall realize and live in the possession of that highest good to which the holy life conducts us and for the sake of which youths of good family so nobly retire from the household life to the houseless one." The Bhikkhus listened, and they were converted by listening to the Doctrine of the Noble Eightfold Way. For three months the Blessed One sojourned at Isipatana, and within that time received into His new Religion sixty Bhikkhus, and to these sixty emancipated ones the Blessed One gave the Order "Wander O ye Bhikkhus, and proclaim the Doctrine of Threefold Glory, for the welfare and happiness of men and gods. In compassion to the world preach this Doctrine glorious. Let not two of you go in one direction. Preach the Dhamma to all. For ye have won freedom from lust, ignorance and ill-will."

This wonderful Doctrine, so supreme, so hard to comprehend, not to be understood by mere logical argumentation, only to be comprehended by the wise, and the world so much enveloped in sensuality and pleasure, will they receive it? Would it not be well if I silently pass away without putting myself into inconvenience?" Such a thought flashed forth, and the god Brahma appearing before the Blessed One, paying homage solicited Him, that the Doctrine should be proclaimed for there were beings prepared to listen, and the Blessed One thereupon looked through the world, and found that there were beings sufficiently developed to comprehend the sublime Doctrine.

The Buddha was a Prince of the royal Rajput clan, and there were at the time other Indian teachers, to wit, Purana Kasyapa, Makkhali Gosala, Pakuda Katyayana, Ajita Kesakambala, Sanjaya Belattiputta, and Niganta Natha Putra who were each with large followings wandering through the Gangetic valley, proclaiming to the people that what each one had found was the absolute truth, and that other systems were false. These were heterodox doctrines unsuited to the genius of the Aryan people, and the Magadha people were looking for a great teacher, and the World Physician appeared with the panacea of the Middle Doctrine, sweet in the beginning, sweet in the middle, sweet in the end, the complete fulfilment of the Brahmachariya Doctrine. He was only thirty-five years—the Blessed One—when He began to proclaim the Doctrine, and the whole of the Magadha, Kasi, Kosala, Anga, Kuru, and Mithila country were in expectation of the appearance of the majestic personality who was dressed in the Bhikkhu garb of yellow, with bowl in hand, of incomparable mien, His voice that of the kuravika bird, so penetrating and yet so melodious, that even the animals and birds became calm—and there was not one in all India to appear before Him to contradict what He uttered. The all-illuminating Sun He was, at whose radiance minor lights of territorial teachers lost their splendour. With a following of 1,250 Bhikkhus, He marched forth from kingdom to kingdom, the kings, princes, barons, of each province extending their hospitality to the Blessed One. The king of Magadha, the king of Kosala, the Brahmans of Mithila, the Mallian Princes and others became His lay disciples. The 1,000 Jatila ascetics of Uruvela, Nadi and Gaya with their chiefs, of the family of Kassapa, became His Bhikkhu disciples. His two chief disciples, Sariputra and Maudgalyana were, of the Brahman gotra and the principal Bhikkhu disciples were mostly of the Kshatriya and Brahman castes. Sons of the several highest baronial families like Ratthapala, Yasa, Sona, renounced their wealth and joined the Bhikkhu order. Bhikshinis from the royal and other castes were proclaiming the Dharma. The young Religion was converting the people by the thousands, and men, women and children were drinking the ambrosia of the immortal Dharma. Brahman ministers of the Kosalan and Magadhan kings were willing to acknowledge the Blessed One as their Guru. The Itivuttaka, one of the minor portions of the Khuddaka Nikaya, gives us portions of "Thus saith the Blessed One," wherein we find His especial *logia*, and in one of the *vuttam hetam* is His solicitude for the Brahman: "Bahupakara Bhikkhave Brahmanagahapatika" wherein the Bhikkhus are especially enjoined to minister unto the Brahman householders by preaching to them the Dharma, for they give unto the Bhikkhus robes, food, seats, etc. The Blessed One was the friend of all, and the sacrificing and caste Brahmans were offended and became hostile to Him for no other reason except that He preached against animal sacrifices and rituals as well as on the oneness of humanity. He combated the idea of the creationists who enunciated the teleological principle that the Brahmans came from the mouth of the Brahma. A special first creation out of nothing, and a special caste created by Brahma, with special privileges to trample on the rights of the Kshatriya, Vaishya and Sudra were what the compassionate Lord could not accept. He enunciated the biological law of cellular development culminating in the gradual evolution of the foetus in the human womb. He saw no special caste in the embryo. Ethnologically there was no differentiation in the human embryo, and in man differentiation is ethical. He who does good deeds he is the Brahman, he who does evil deeds he is the barbarian. It is association and environment that influence the development, or the retardation of the human being. What we eat, where we live, the water that we drink, have all to be considered as factors in the evolution of life. Association with unenlightened, savage people leads one to the wrong path. The acceptance of the Law of cause and effect gives man the enlightenment to analyse and differentiate the good from the evil. It is not what you believe, but what you think, speak and act that influences the being, either for good or for evil. Good thoughts, good speech, good acts help the individual in progressive evolution. Man retrogades according to his thoughts if they are evil. Thought is chiefly responsible for our actions; loving thoughts help our evolutionary progress; cruel, angry thoughts retard our growth.

Buddha the Enlightened One came to the world to show the path of Righteousness, to destroy the path of error. Animistic religions, teach erroneous doctrines of a special creation, a predestined fatalism as well as annihilation. A creator creating matter connotes a beginning while the Buddha taught that there could be no beginning, and no annihilation. Law guides the intelligent, rational being and to depend on somebody else is to run after a will'o-the-wisp. We know that enlightenment came to the world by investigation not by prayer, nor by ritualistic practices, nor by animal sacrifices. The Blessed One found the cause of human suffering, and He found the fetters that have enchained man. In the discovery that He made He brought light to the world. For two thousand years Europe lived in darkness, and with the enunciation of the Darwinian theory of evolution with its corollary, the Law of cause and effect, Europe began to make giant strides. Hygiene, Sanitation, Astronomy, Biology, Electricity, Geology, Paleontology, etc., have helped the progress of the world in the physical plane. Ecclesiasticism was based on metaphysical delusion, and from this hydra-headed monster arose false beliefs. Consciousness works according to environment. Its development depends on nutrition, physically, and psychically. Good, nourishing food helps the development of the body, and a well developed body naturally produces a healthy brain. The starving, famished individual cannot evolve high thoughts. Existence depends on food, consciousness, contact and individualising thought. Consciousness is of three kinds, *viz.*, low, middling and high. Those of the material plane, who think only of self and of material food belong to the low plane; those who think of self and a material heaven belong to the middle plane; and those who think altruistically, forgetting self, and working for the welfare of others without thought of the ego are of the exalted plane.

Unfortunately for the welfare of the world, Buddhism which flourished in India as the national religion lost its place in India in the 12th century and with the so-called revival of Brahmanism the Dharma was forgotten. With the advent of the British power the vestiges of ancient Buddhism began to speak, and antiquarians and archæologists commenced their work of exploration. Now that the whole world, especially Asia, is in a state of ferment, there is some hope that Buddhism will find followers in the West as well as in India. It all depends on the intellectual progress that the people make in the domain of religion. If they are contented with ceremonies, rituals, speculations, metaphysics, magic, etc., Buddhism will find no place in their heart. But in place of superstition when there arises a desire for investigation, analysis, and a scepticism there is hope for the Dharma. It is only when people are yearning for something better than what they have that their wishes find consummation. Sensuality and a scepticism are the two extremes that the Enlightened One wished that the searcher after Truth should avoid. Sensualism begets the delusion of an ego-eternalism, and asceticism begets pride, ignorance and false belief. What Buddha wished to destroy from the mind of the Brahmachari was the seed of egoism and craving for sensual enjoyment. The highest happiness which is realizable here, in perfect consciousness, is obtainable by the effort of man, provided that he walks in the Middle Path which is the Path of Immortality. Evil leads to destruction and evil is opposed to Nirvana. Every effort to destroy Covetousness, Anger, Delusion or Ignorance is good, it is a stepping stone to Nirvana. There are the good desires and evil desires, desires that give pain to self or others, are evil; desires that produce mental peace and happiness and enlightenment are good, for they bring one nearer to Nirvana. Sankharas are of three kinds, the good, the bad, and the neutral.

To develop good Sankharas we have to make the effort to practise certain good qualities, as for instance, faith, charity, listening to wisdom's lore, persevering in effort, and acquiring higher knowledge. To be born in heaven is good, and the aspiration is a good Sankhara, to be born a king is a good Sankhara, to be born in a noble family is a good Sankhara, and to realize the ideal it is necessary to make the effort. Selfish, sensual desires of a low kind belong to the plane of low Sankharas. For further knowledge on this subject the reader is referred to the Sankharuppatti sutta of the Majjhima nikaya.

Speculation is condemned as useless, for it is time wasted to think of things that are immeasurable, as for instance, a man trying to compute the sands of the Ganges, or to weigh the waters of the great oceans. This sort of speculation, it is said, may lead man to insanity. The ocean is there, but if we go to make the effort to weigh its waters, the effort is futile, and time is wasted, which could have been spent otherwise for the good of self and others. Prayer is useless, for what is required is effort. The time spent on prayer is lost, and the time spent on effort to achieve something is not lost. Concentration is most necessary, such as bringing all good thoughts into a focus. This is called Samadhi. Mental illumination is called Dhyana. It is a condition that has to be got at by refraining from all sensuality and evil (kama and akusalas), and making the effort in the path of good, by investigation, research, and discrimination. Dhyana is not trance but spiritual psychic illumination. The cessation of feeling and perception is called nirodha samapatti, which is possible only to the absolutely pure Brahmachari, of the Anagami order. Dhyana is within the reach of cosmic psychology, and the ordinary Brahmacharis can reach the four stages of cosmic Dhyana, but the *nirodha* is of the supercosmic kind and only Anagamis and Arhats can realize the state by walking in the Eightfold Noble Path.

## SKANDHAS

The changing personality according to the psychology of Buddha is made up of the five Skandhas. The individualised entity as such does not exist permanently for two consecutive moments. Sankharas are changing like the flame of a lamp, or the flowing water of a stream. The stream of consciousness flows on unceasingly, and the thoughts generated continues on, life to life, now in heaven, now on earth, now as a god, now as a human being, now in the form of an animal, now as a sub-human being, by the force of karma generated in previous lives. " I think egoistically, therefore I am " and this feeling and this sensation are the effects of Ignorance. Happiness is to refrain from engendering Sankharas of either good, bad or neutral, and to live in the sphere of Pragna in the domain of Nirvanic Wisdom.

In the words of the gifted author of " Buddhist Psychological Ethics "—" the pre-Buddhist Upanishads (and those, too, of later date) yield only poetic adumbrations, sporadic aphorisms on the work of the senses. The Nyaya doctrine of pratyaksha or perception, the Jaina sutras, the elaboration of the Vedantic and Sankhya doctrines are, of course, of far later date.".........Buddhism preached a doctrine of regenerate personality, to be sought after and developed by and out of, the personal resources of the individual through a system of intellectual self culture." The Buddha having won the Great Freedom from all cosmic sensations and perceptions, willingly and compassionately opened the "Door of Immortality" to all who were inclined to enter the kingdom of Brahmachariya.

Buddhism may be called the Religion of Analysis. It analyses every phase of cosmic phenomenon, the constituents that go to make up the human being, and the differentiating states of mentality; it categorises the differentiation of Good, Evil and Neutral; it rejects every phase of superstitious belief that is based on mere tradition, speculations, revelation, magic, analogy, logic, authority and collected discourses, and appeals to the purified heart to distinguish the good from the bad, and to avoid doing anything that is correlated with covetousness, anger and lust. All that is pure, and free from covetousness, anger and lust are productive of good, and therefore to be acted upon. Such was the doctrine that the Blessed One enunciated to the chiefs of the Kalama country which is elucidated in detail in the Kalama sutta of the Anguttara nikaya.

Critics, especially students of Sanskrit, followers of Vedanta, fail to understand correctly the psychology of the Dharma as enunciated by the Tathagato. They try to interpret the religion of the Buddha not as it is understood by the orthodox followers of the Pali Buddhism, but as understood by them, according to their Vedantic knowledge. The result is that they succeed in misleading the unenlightened. Christian propagandists in Buddhist countries have been guilty of misrepresentation in that they have misled European people to believe that Buddhism is pessimism as well as nihilism. Nirvana is the *summum bonum* of Buddhism; the culmination of all the virtues, of charity, self-sacrifice, morality, enlightenment, righteous endeavour, truthfulness, forgiveness, patience, resoluteness, will-power to do the right thing, love, kindness, compassion, mercy, cheerfulness, scientific investigation, serenity, renunciation of sensuality awakefulness, faith begotten of knowledge, and the realisation of absolute freedom, which are synonymous with Nirvana, to the muddle-headed appears as something to be shunned. And for proclaiming this most subtle doctrine the Buddha Sakya Muni, the Blessed Tathagato is blamed !

## THE GOSPEL OF DESTRUCTION

Buddhism disappears when its followers turn away from the Path of enlightenment and follow other pagan gods and a code of immoral ethics. Man is more inclined to follow the sensual path than the path of ethical purity. Buddhism insists that its followers should abstain from destruction of life, but the heathenish diabolisms preached by brutal savages proclaim the gospel of destruction. In these days of brute force backed up by Krupp guns, and Dum-Dum bullets, and sharpnels, the doctrine of compassion and the gospel of renunciation can make very little headway, even in lands where it has taken root. Buddhism prohibits alcoholic drinks and drugs, and in Ceylon where the religion has flourished for nearly 2,100 years, since the British advent, we see all old traditions being wiped off by the introduction of Western abominations. Daily papers in that island published by the Christians contain advertisements by the column singing the glories of Johnny Walker's Whisky, D.C.L. Whisky, Dewar's Whisky, White Horse Whisky, House of Lords Whisky, King George's Whisky, Breadlebane's Whisky; and in a country where the religion of the rulers teaches that God's flesh and blood are believed to be taken to gain admission to a mythical heaven, where angels in goose wings sing eternal hallulujahs, a pure religion suited to the purified nature of the Aryans could not exist. Consequently we see the noble Religion of the Tathagato slowly disappearing from the island where it had so long flourished. There is no way to prevent it, and as long as the religion of the pagans influences the Sinhalese Buddhists, so long will Buddhism decline and not prosper. For what is immoral in Buddhism is considered moral in pagan religions.

In India Buddhism flourished under kings like Asoka and Siladitya and Mahipala and others, and it began to decline when the people began to turn their attention to sensual enjoyments. A virile people determined to reach the highest realms of truth and righteousness were the ancient Indian people, and for nearly 1,500 years they kept Buddhism as a kind of national heirloom. But when the cohorts of Mahmud of Ghazni commenced their savage vandalism, and persisted in their savage career under successive iconoclasts, extending for several centuries, Buddhism ceased to exist. Buddhism is only fit for a people that cherish righteousness, not for savages who love to live in destruction and bacchanalian revelry. The Bactrain Buddhists deviated from the teachings of Buddha, and Buddhists of the mediæval period began to make compromises with the theosophic scholasticism of the Brahmans. The purified ethics and the uncompromising psychology of the Anatman doctrine were neglected and a degenerating ritual was introduced which helped to hypnotise the people by its glamour, but in reality helped to accentuate the destruction of the vitalising Dharma. It was like the decrease of the reverberating sound of the drum whose rim when embellished with jewels and gems, results in the resonating sound being lost. The Buddha had foretold that His Religion would decline with the increase of ceremonialism introduced by a luxurious priesthood, in the Kassapa Samyutta, Sanyutta nikaya.

### THE ESSENTIALS OF THE RELIGION

To say that Buddha borrowed His religion from the Vedas and the pantheistic Upanishads and Kapila sutras would be like saying that Darwin borrowed his philosophy from the Christian Bible and the Aristotlean ethics, and that Herbert Spencer got his philosophy from the treatises of mediæval theologians. If what Buddha had declared was only a rehash of Brahmanical dishes it would have never become the religion of the vigorous Asoka. Buddhism is both vigorous and puritanic, and as such an effeminate people cannot maintain it, and a people addicted to sensuality cannot adhere to its virile, purifying ethics.

The doctrine of Anatman enunciated by the Buddha has been a bugbear to the spiritualist, pantheist, and monotheist. Do I exist? Did I exist? Shall I exist? Is the Ego different from the body, or are they both identical? Do they exist in a permanent form? Or do they become extinct? Such kind of speculative questions the Blessed One has relegated to the limbo of oblivion. He considered all such questions to be out of court. There is no agnosticism in Buddhism. The truth asbolute the Buddha has proclaimed, and that is, that absolute Wisdom culminating in the blessedness and peace of Nirvana could be realized in this life in perfect consciousness, without having recourse to the foolish speculations of the Whence and the Whither and the What, am I? Neither a belief in a Creator, nor the acceptance of a fatalistic determinism, nor the rejection of a future life are considered as essentials for the realization of the perfect state. The metaphysics of religion are unnecessary adjuncts. They are considered as fetters, and the essentials of animistic beliefs have to be utterly abandoned. Primitive savages worshipped the wind god, the rain god, the thunder god, the sun god, the water god, and when they became enlightened and knew how to construct houses and protect themselves from rain and wind and sun, the gods became useless. When Darwin propounded the theory of evolution the theologians were frightened and they all shouted that Darwin had killed the Creator! The principle now accepted by the thinking people that nothing is lost, and that causes produce effects, which again become the nucleus of a cause is a rational doctrine: but very few really take it seriously. The old faith is easy, and no effort is made to be good, and like the man given to alcoholic drink and opium, he clings to it, however pernicious they are for the moral well-being of man. Habit plays an important part in the acceptance and rejection of rational and irrational beliefs. In India re-marriage of virgin widows is considered a crime, and any effort made to prevent infant marriages is considered an interference of religion. In European countries beef-eating is a necessity, while in India it is a crime to kill the cow. Asceticism is a form of religious vow in certain religions, but is rejected by the Blessed One as utterly useless. The belief in an ego is a fetter that binds man into a heresy, and the disciple of Buddha has to make a studious effort to get rid of the error. The object of the great Teacher was to make all beings happy, and the principal idea that keeps human beings separate is the heresy of a permanent ego-personality, clinging to certain sensations and perceptions, and in the desire to have them permanently, foolish efforts are made which end in strife, creating differences between father and son, between brother and brother, between sister and sister, between sister and brother, between mother and daughter. This pernicious doctrine is called in the religion of Buddha, *tanha mana-ditthi* ; another name for which is *ahamkara-mamamkara.* As long as this insane idea works in the mind, so long is there no emancipation for him from the fetters of craving desire. The simple question that we have to ask ourselves is, is it advantageous to give pain to another? Monotheistic faiths declare that the Creator having created animals for food, it is our duty to the Creator to give him thanks and kill and eat the animals! This absolutely savage doctrine when carried to its logical conclusion lands us in the domain of cannibalism. The god of the cannibal has declared to him that the flesh of the white man may be eaten, and the tiger by the instinct implanted in its animal brain by the Creator seeks its prey in a helpless cow! But man who is the owner of a gun and who believes in a creator would find no comfort unless he was successful in destroying the tiger! Fatalists believe that whatever happens has been pre-ordained by the Creator, and to accept everything with resignation is considered faithfulness to God. Nevertheless, fatalists do make the exertion to realise the consummation of their cherished desires. The nihilists who reject both the theories yet make the exertion to enjoy the materialistic pleasures possible to obtain in this life. Exertion is therefore very material, whatever the belief one may entertain and the one who does not make the endeavour fails to achieve the desired goal. This righteous endeavour is sammappadhana. Exertion to achieve that which would give no happiness to others is called micchavayamo. Delay to exert to do the right thing is conducive to evil, and dependence on others is against the law of development. Each man is the maker of his own destiny, and the evil that one does continues to bring unhappiness to the world till its effects are neutralised by good deeds. The Blessed One by His great illuminating insight discovered this most wonderful doctrine whereby man was given the power to make the effort to realize the goal of perfect freedom.

### THE DECLINE OF BUDDHISM

India was great for 1,500 years, and the decline began from the time that the Bhikkhus and lay followers neglected the observance of the great Law of Purity and the study of Psychical Science.

### THE ETHICS OF RIGHTEOUSNESS

The first five principles of ethics that were enunciated by the Tathagato belong to the domain of politics. In the Cakkavatti sutta, Digha Nikaya, it is said that the King-

Emperor of India instituted the five laws for the welfare of the people of the land, and these the Blessed One reinstituted for the welfare of the whole world, and these five rules became the guiding light of the followers of the Tathagato. They are :—

I pledge to observe the precept of avoiding destruction of life.

I pledge to observe the precept of refraining from taking other's property.

I pledge to observe the precept of refraining from sexual immorality.

I pledge to observe the precept of refraining from lying, harsh speech, slander, etc.

I pledge to observe the precept of refraining from taking alcoholic drinks and stupifying drugs which tend to decay. These five precepts are for the daily use of the householders.

The Buddha classified the ethical rules into the cosmic and supercosmic. The one to the category of the heavenly ethics and the other to the Nirvana. The popular gatha summarises Buddhist ethics thus :—

Sabbapapassa akaranam, Kusalassa upasampada

Sachitta pariyodapanam, etam Buddha-nasasanam.

Let no evil be done, let good deeds be replenished. Let one's heart be purified, these are the exhortations of the Buddha.

The ten evils which are to be avoided are called dasa akusala, *viz.*, three of the body, four of speech, three of the mind.

Three of the body are :—not to kill ; not to steal, not to do deeds of sexual and sensual immorality : four of the speech are :—not to tell lies, not to slander, nor to use harsh speech, or unprofitable talk ; three of the mind are :—covetousness, ill-will, and clinging to unscientific views, denying the law of cause and effect, now and hereafter.

The positive rules of ethical conduct are dana, sila bhavana, veyyavaccha, apachayana, pattipattanu modana, dhamma savana and dhammadesana, ditthiujjukata.) Gifts and charities, purifying moral conduct; thinking of good things; serving others in accordance with the rules of decorum, nursing the sick and elders, etc.; asking others to share with us in doing good, giving the merits of one's good deeds to others, hearing the Good Law, preaching the Good Law, strengthening one's views according to the law of causality.

### THE BRAHMACHARI LIFE.

In Buddhism householders are expected to practise lessons of self-abnegation as well as the rules of Brahmachariya. The Brahmacharis alone are expected to realize the state of Nirvana. The way to Nirvana is one, the way of the worldly is another. Renunciation and Brahmachariya constitute the attributes of the Nirvana life. The good householder, whether man or woman is expected to lead the holy life once in a week according to the changes of the moon. On the fullmoon day it is said that the celestial beings visit the earth to witness the performance of good deeds by the upasakas and upasikas. On the fullmoon day the messengers of Indra with the golden book in hand go about recording the good deeds of human beings as it is mentioned in the Devaduta sutta. Yama is the God of Judgment according to popular Buddhism, and he judges each individual according to the karma, whether good or bad. Karma is the act, and karma is of three kinds, *viz.*, good, bad or neutral. In consciousness karma is done, and any act deliberately done is called a karma. (Cetanayam bhikkhave kammam vadami). We reap what we have sown, and what we now sow we shall reap in after times. The good or bad things that we enjoy without effort is the result of the karma of the past. And every deed now done, whether good or bad, deliberately, becomes a karma for future fruition. Powerful karma takes precedence in their fruition. The acceptance of the doctrine of Karma (Pali: Kamma) connotes the acceptance of the idea of rebirth, *viz.*, that the individual being now living is a link in the chain of existences. It means that the individual was not for the first time created by a Creator or a Supreme Lord, but that he is a sentient being without a known beginning, and without end. The limitless past is beyond our ken, but we know that we exist because we think and go through sensations and perceptions; and the future is beyond us, and we do not know whether we shall live to-morrow, but that this moment now that is ours, we shall do good without delay for the realization of the highest happiness. The gods exist as sentient beings in the celestial regions, but they too are under the law of causality. Some day they too die. And the human being that is given to do good deeds, and leads the purifying Brahmachariya life is greater than the celestial gods. The Uposatha life is as follows :—

I abstain from destroying life,

I abstain from taking other's things,

I abstain from every phase of sexuality,

I abstain from falsehood,

I abstain from taking intoxicants, etc.,

I abstain from eating food after the sun passes the meridian,

I abstain from dancing, singing sensual music, shows, wearing garlands, scents, etc.,

I abstain from using high and luxurious beds.

The Brahmachariya life has variations. One can lead the consecrated life of purity by observing the rules except the one relating to taking food at unseasonable hours. The Brahmachariya life is also necessary for the psychical researchers if they wish to realize the higher laws of psychicism. Buddhism admits the potentialities of the purified consciousness. The uncontaminated life is capable of doing marvellous deeds, known as the miraculous. Divine hearing surpassing the hearing of men and divine sight looking back to past births, reading other's thoughts, acquiring wonder-working powers, are the fruitions of the purified life of earnest, truthful, upright, men and women. Psychicism is a very fertile field in Buddhist psychology. The very elaborate work called the Visuddhi Marga deals abundantly on the subject of psychical research.

The student Brahmachari who is willing to walk in the path of Nirvana has to put on the armour of Righteousness known as the Bodhi pakkhiya dhamma. He has to know thoroughly the thirty seven principles of the Bodhi *viz.*,

the four satipatthanas,

the four earnest endeavours,

the four psychical foundations,
the five psychical sense organs,
the five psychical powers,
the seven principles of wisdom,
the eightfold noble path.

ANALYSIS

The four satipatthanas deal with the five skhandhas under four categories whereby psychical attentiveness is resolutely fixed on the Nirvana plane. Physiologically, biologically, and psychologically, the constituents of the body have to be analysed, thereby knowledge is gained about the transitoriness of the physical form, the variations of the threefold sensations showing their transitory nature, as well as the transitory nature of the volitions of the consciousness and the impediments that are called Nirvanas, *viz.*, desire for sensual enjoyment, ill-will and anger, mental lethargy, irritability and scepticism based on ignorance. To fix the mind resolutely on the Nirvanic state, the complex variations of the body, sensations and volitions must be brought under control, being purified from the dross born of sexual passions, anger, indolence, excitability and erring doubt. The Satipatthana sutta of the Digha Nikaya translated by Rhys Davids in the "Dialogues of the Buddha" may be usefully studied to comprehend the essential features of the psychical science of the Tathagato.

Buddhism is the Religion of Earnest unswerving Effort. It looks to no god, or gods and asks for no extraneous help except that of one's own purity of conduct and unselfness. "Look to no extraneous aid, make yourself an island, depend on none, depend on the strength of your own righteous exertions, and the supreme effort made with earnestness to control the low nature is sure to succeed. Strive earnestly, make the earnest endeavour, persevere strenuously, let no lethargy and irritability and scepticism prevent you from reaching the goal. Ring out the old, ring in the new, avoid evil, store in the good. Fight valiantly against sin and lust and selfishness."

Buddhism teaches that man can attain Nirvana in this life but he must stand on the foundations of Iddhipada, and develop the five psychic organs, *viz.*, faith, attentiveness, indomitable energy, concentration of good thoughts, and of wisdom. He has to develop the seven attributes of supreme wisdom, *viz.*, psychical attentiveness, analysis of the skhandhas, elements of being, seats of consciousness, the law of cause and effect based on the law of Dependent Origination which are called the Nidanas. He must strenuously exert with indomitable will-power, he must be always cheerful, serene, and practise the power of concentration, and show that spirit of loving equanimity for all living beings. With this armour he must be prepared to walk in the Eightfold Noble Path which is the absolute way to reach the goal of Nirvana in this life. The eight principles are:

Right knowledge of the existence of suffering, the origin thereof, its cessation and the way to cease, these constitute right knowledge together with the grasping of the law of Dependent Origination beginning with Ignorance.

Right Aspirations cherishing the desire to be merciful to all, to love all, and to make the renunciation of sensual pleasures.

Right Speech which encourageth loving and truthful speech.

Right Actions which consist of observing the precepts relating to non-destruction of life, not stealing, and abstinence from sensual immorality.

Right Livelihood in that whereby no life is destroyed, no alcohol nor poision is given, and no profession of destruction is adopted.

Right Endeavour to give up evil, and to develop the good.

Right Attention or Mindfulness whereby the Consciousness is fixed on Nirvana abandoning all sensations and perceptions.

Right Samadhi whereby the four Illuminations are realised and Nirvana reached in perfect Consciousness.

THE FOUR STAGES OF HOLINESS

The disciple of the Tathagato who is making the strenuous exertion to reach the goal of Nirvana should have supreme faith in Him, in the doctrine that He taught, and in the Holy Ones who had reached the supreme condition of Arhatship. The paths are four and the fruits of holiness are four. The Sotapatti path and its fruition, the Sakadagami path and its fruition, the Anagami path and its fruition, the Arhat path and its fruition. The four attributes of the Sotapatti student are association with the righteous, hearing the good law, thinking from cause to effect, and observing the laws of truth and purity. The Sotapatti student must give up attachment to self, should have no wavering doubt, and must be free from ritualistic ceremonies. The Sotapatti is unswerving in his purifying life. He never deviates from the path of perfect rectitude. He is free from destructive tendencies, is never dishonest, never indulges in unlawful sexuality, never speaks an untruth, and never takes intoxicants. The Sakadagami has destroyed the above and is trying to attenuate his passions tending towards anger, ill-will, hatred and passionate lust. The Anagami has destroyed all the above and is free from passion and anger. The Arhat has destroyed the above as well as the other five fetters, *viz.*, desire for heavenly rupa and arupa births, conceit, irritability and all round delusion. He is without desires; and the fear of old age, decay and death has been destroyed. His consciousness has gone beyond the realms of rupa, arupa and kama. He has transcended the condition of gods and men.

# THE ARYA DHARMA AND THE COMING OF THE BUDDHA OF LOVE

The present kalpa is called the great good kalpa, inasmuch as four Buddhas had already appeared, and the fifth is expected when the new race appears. The present race will continue to deteriorate, righteousness will gradually disappear; injustice, deviation from the path of truth, covetousness, unnatural lust, cruelty will continue to increase. The Kaliyuga according to the Puranas will last for another 250,000 years, and then will begin the dawn of the new manvantara. But according to Buddhist eschatalogy the present race will gradually decline and the race destroyed by various cataclysms, and the remnants of the race will be the nucleus of the new race that will be reborn.

Those that are now walking in the path of righteousness showing mercy to all, abstaining from hurting others, from stealing, from committing adultery, from falsehood, from drinking intoxicating drinks, from following the vicious methods of false teachers, will after death be reborn in the Tusita heaven where the future Buddha is now living.

The next Buddha will be born in the Brahman caste, and the city of his birth will be Benares, which will then be called Ketumati. The age of the people who are born then will be very long, and only righteousness will reign. There will be no killing, stealing and committing adultery, no untruth, no drinking of liquor, no nakedness, no poverty, no mud houses, no filth, no dirt, the cities will be all lighted, and parks, and gardens abound. It will be a heaven on earth.

Those who are now doing good work, and showing kindness to parents, to elders, and to holy men and good Brahmans, and abstain from killing animals, who do not follow heretical doctrines, who do not follow the path of naked ascetics, who do not rub ash on their bodies, who give charity to the poor, who follow the doctrine of karma, and who accept the doctrine of rebirth will after death be reborn in the Tusita heaven.

When the new earth and the new race are born the Buddha Maittreyya, the Lord of Love, will be reborn in Benares. Those who are now doing good works, with faith in the Buddha and those who had already been dead after having done good work; their place is Tusita. All good Buddhists who had failed to enter one of the four paths of holiness under the Dispensation of the Gautama Buddha will become the disciples of the Lord of Love. For another two thousand and five hundred years the message of the coming Lord will be heard. The yellow robed Bhikkhus will continue to announce the message of deliverance.

The Buddha Gautama in the sermon that He delivered to Bhikkhus called the Cakkavatti sutta, Majjhima nikaya, proclaimed the coming of the great Lord of Love.

Every Buddha teaches the following principles of the Arya Dhamma. The righteous king, the great universal emperor, Raja Chakravarti, rules his empire by the power of righteousness. He is the first to proclaim the ten daily rules for the observance of his people, *viz.*, to abstain from cruelty and destruction of life, from stealing, from committing adultery, from falsehood, foul speech, slander, and intoxicating drinks and drugs, ill-will, covetousness and unbelief. The righteous emperor doth see that every one in his empire is not burdened with poverty; he provides the poor with means, and sees that they are able to gain their livelihood by honest labour and industrial pursuits; he exhorts the people that they should take care of their parents and elders in the family and honour and entertain holy Brahmans and holy Sramanas.

When a perfect all-enlightened Buddha appears, and no two Buddhas appear at the same time, He teaches the five Chakravarti rules for daily observance, and also the ten meritorious deeds, *viz.*, Charity to observe the rules of moral conduct, to practise the development of good thoughts, to honour and to attend to the comforts of parents and teachers and nurse them when they are sick, to show hospitality to strangers, to ask others to share in the good work that one is doing, to accept the share in the good work that others are doing, to preach the Good Law, and to hear the Good Law, and to keep one's faith upright.

On the fullmoon days of each month the householder is expected to observe the rules of Brahmachari life in abstaining from sexual intercourse, from eating at unseasonable hours, and going to places of immoral amusements and dancing parties. On that day he has to abstain from all kinds of luxurious seats, clothes, scents, perfumes, etc.

The three paths to Nirvana are: samma-sambodhi, pratyeka bodhi, and sravaka bodhi The first is the supreme, the second is middling, and the third is low. The Mahayana path is the path of the supreme bodhisatvas who aspire to become Buddhas, the Majjhima or Ekayana path is for the pratyeka Buddhas, and the hinayana path is for those who wish to enter Nirvana quicker without concerning about the salvation of others. The hinayana bodhisatvas follow a perfect Buddha, inasmuch as they are unable to discover the Four

Truths by their own efforts. The Pratyeka bodhisatvas do not want the help of a perfect Buddha, and they discover the path, but they are unable to proclaim the Truths to others. The pratyeka Buddhas invariably appear when no fully enlightened Buddhas appear. The hinayana sravaka bodhisatvas are born only when an all-enlightened Buddha appears. They become Arhantas and attain Nirvana on this earth. To attain arhatship the ten paramitas have to be practised for one asankheyya kalpa; to become a pratyeka Buddha for two asankheyya kalpas; to become an all-enlightened Buddha for four asankheyya and one hundred thousand kalpas. The ten paramitas are Charity absolute and universal; Moral conduct in perfection; Renunciation of sensual pleasures and aspiring to holiness; Observing the path of Wisdom supreme; Strenuous Exertion to reach the goal; unfaltering Truthfulness; Forgiving patience; Indomitable Will to reach the Consummation; Universal love to all living creatures; Indifference to praise and blame in the performance of duty.

## THE PRINCIPAL DOCTRINES OF THE DHARMA

*The Four Satipatthanas : Thought Fixities.*

Analysis of the Breath and the 32 Categories of the Body.

Analysis of Sense Feelings.

Analysis of ideations (chittas).

Analysis of the five psychical hindrances and of the seven principles of Enlightenment (bojjhangas).

*The Four Samyak Pradhana : Right Exertions.*

Exertion to destroy evil thoughts already arisen.

Exertion to prevent Evil thoughts arising.

Exertion to originate meritorious thoughts.

Exertion to develop and increase meritorious thoughts already arisen.

*The Four Iddhipadas : Bases of Working Wonders.*

Intense desire to acquire psychical powers and Nirvana.

The strenuous energy to acquire good karma for the development of psychical powers.

Development of meritorious thoughts.

Investigation and analysis of the methods adopted.

*The Five Indriyas : Seats of Power.*

Faith, Power of Recollection, Strenuous Energy, Psychical Concentration, and Wisdom supreme.

*The Five Bala : Psychical Powers.*

Power of Faith, Power of Recollection, Power of Energy, Power of Psychical Concentration. Power of Supernal Wisdom.

*The Seven Constituents of Perfect Enlightenment : Bojjhangas.*

1. Recollection of the four Contents relating to the formation of the body, sense feelings, ideations, and psychical hindrances and helps.
2. Investigation of the psychical categories of the four noble truths, the thought fixities, indriyas, balas, bojjhangas.
3. Undaunted energy, strenuous exertion to reach the goal.
4. Cheerfulness without hilarity.
5. Serenity and composure of body.
6. Concentration of meritorious thoughts.
7. Equalmindedness, indifference to praise and blame.

### *The Noble Eightfold Path: Ariya Maggangani.*

1. Right views opposed to nihilistic and unscientific views.

2. Right desires of mercy, loving kindness, and renunciation of sense pleasures.

3. Right Speech, truthfulness, abstaining from slander, harsh speech, and idle talk.

4. Right Actions—abstinence from destruction of life, stealing; committing adultery and sexual indulgence, and drinking intoxicants.

5. Right Livelihood; abstaining from the five sinful professions of slave dealing, selling poisons, intoxicants of all kinds, flesh of animals, and murderous weapons.

6. Right Exertion. Exertion to destroy evil thoughts already arisen, Exertion to prevent evil thoughts arising, Exertion to originate meritorious thoughts, Exertion to expand, develop and increase meritorious thoughts already arisen.

7. Right Mindfulness: to analyse the inhalations and exhalations of one's breath, and to analyse the 32 components of the body; to analyse the differentiating sense feelings; to

analyse the manifold arisings of the heart; to analyse the five psychical hindrances, and the seven principles of enlightenment.

8. Right Psychical Illuminations. The practise of the first, second, third and fourth dhyanas to realize Nirvana.

*The Five Psychical Hindrances: Nivaranas.*

Desire for sexual enjoyment; Ill-will, hatred, anger; Sleepiness, Laziness; Mind-wanderings, restlessness; Scepticism based on nihilism.

*The Twelve Nidanas: Basic Elements Operating Interdependently Causing Rebirth.*

1. Ignorance (Avidya) of the 24 Laws of Cause and Effect.

2. Thought Ideations producing karma (Sankharas).

3. Cognitions depending on ideations (Vinnana).

4. Mind activities and correlative formation of the physical body (Namarupa).

5. Activities of the six sense organs (Salayatana).

6. Contact produced by activities of the Consciousness depending on objective phenomena with the six sense organs (Phasso).

7. Feelings produced by the sixfold Contact (Vedana).

8. The Intense Craving for sexual and sensual pleasures of the material and heavenly planes (Tanha).

9. Psychological Bases of Rebirth which are foolish ascetic habits, retention of the erroneous idea of a permanent ego, desire for sense pleasures in a heavenly form, holding erroneous beliefs (Upadana).

10. Re-birth (Realms of Existences) in the Kama, Rupa, and Arupa lokas (Bhavo).

11. The Coming together of the five Skhandhas resulting in individualized rebirth (Jati).

12. Decay, Dissolution of the body called death, grief, lamentation, despair, (jara, marana, soka, parideva, dukkha, domanassa, upayasa).

*The Twelve Nidanas Classified into Seven Categorical Groups.*

*First Group*: Consists of Nidanas of Ignorance, Ideations, Cravings, Bases of Rebirth, Rebirth Realms. These nidanas operating in the past life produced karma, which resulted in co-ordination of the nidanas of the present rebirth, which may be called the

*Second Group* : Consisting of the Nidanas of Pratisandhi Vinnana, Rebirth consciousness, Mind-and-body, Six sense organs, Contact and Feelings. The nidanas of the second group forming an individuality produce karma in this present life, form the

*Third Group* : Consisting of the Nidanas : Ignorance, Ideations, Cravings, Bases of Rebirth, and Realms of Rebirth. These nidanas operating produce karma for rebirth in the next life, and their co-ordination go to form the

*Fourth Group* : Consisting of the Nidanas : Conception Consciousness, Mind-and-boby, Six sense organs, Contact and Feelings.

*Fifth Group* : Consists of Nidanas : Ideations and Rebirth Realms of Existences. Ideations produce karma, and karma produce rebirth.

*Sixth Group* : Ignorance, Cravings, Bases of Rebirth, co-ordinating form the field of Contaminations.

*Seventh Group*: Consciousness, Mind-and-body, Six sense organs, Contact, Feelings, are the results of Group Fifth.

*Five Skhandhas.*

Body formed of the four changing bhutas, hardness, wateriness, windiness, and heat, called rupa.

Sense Feelings called Vedana.

Sense Perceptions called Sanna.

Ideations or Karma thoughts called Samkharas.

Cognitions called Vinnana.

*The Ten Fetters : Sanyojanas.*

1. Erroneous ideas of a permanent ego inside the body—sakkaya ditthi.

2. Doubt regarding past, and future worlds, and about the Buddha and Dharma, and unbelief in the law of karma—vicikiccha.

3. Mortifying asceticism in order to gain heavenly reward—silabbata paramasa.

4. Desire for sensual enjoyment in the celestial regions—Kamaraga.

5. Anger, ill-will, hatred—Patigha.

6. Desire to be born in the world of

Brahma and to live permanently there—Ruparaga.

7. Desire to be born in the spiritual world where only the mind exists—Aruparaga.

8. Pride—mana.

9. Vanity—Uddaccha

10. Ignorance of the great law of Casuality and the Four Noble Truths—Avidya.

*The Three Characteristics: Anityam Dukkham, Anatman.*

1. That all forms, sensations, perceptions, ideations, cognitions, subjective and objective, far and near, small and great, invisible and visible, are undergoing change momentarily. This is anityam.

2. That which is subject to change can only produce sorrow, misery, grief. This is dukkha.

3. That which is subject to change, and productive of sorrow: is it wise to say "this is mine," "this is I," and "I am that"? This is Anatman.

*The Three Causes That Produce Demeritorious Karma.*

1. Covetousness, desire for lustful enjoyment.

2. Anger, hatred, ill-will.

3. Muddle-headedness, Ignorance.

The three causes productive of meritorious Karma (1) Non-covetousness (2) Love, kindness, non-anger (3) Wisdom.

*The Seven (Visuddhi) Purities.*

1. The purity in Ethical Conduct.
2. The purity in heart.
3. The purity in religious belief.
4. The purity in having all doubts removed about a future life.
5. The purity in wisdom in knowing the true path and the untrue path.
6. The purity in the knowledge of epistemological science.
7. The purity in the science of wisdom.

*The Seven Steps in the Science of Epistemology.*

1. The science of evolution and dissolution.

2. The science of atomic disintegration.
3. The science of knowing the causes of disintegration.
4. The science of realising the fruits of analysis.
5. The science of knowing that freedom is coming.
6. The science of escaping.
7. The science of thoughtful analysis.
8. The science of analysis of sankharas.
9. The realization of the Noble Truth.

## BUDDHA'S RENUNCIATION *

'My mind is now athirst and longing for the draught of the fountain of sweet dew, saddle then my horse, and quickly bring it here. I wish to reach the deathless city:

'My heart is fixed beyond all change, resolved I am and bound by sacred oath: 'The gates which were before fast-barred and locked, now stand free and open! these evidences of something supernatural point to a climax of my life.'

'Now I desire to fight against and overcome the opposing force of men, the men who associate in search of pleasure, the men who engage in the search after wealth, the crowds who follow and flatter such persons.

'In opposing sorrow, friendly help is difficult (to find), in seeking religious truth there must be rare enlightenment, let us then be knit to-

* Extracts from "The Life of Buddha" by Asvoghosha Bodhisattva.

gether thus as friends; then at last there will be rest from sorrow.

'But now I wish to go abroad to give deliverance from pain; now then, for your own sake it is, and for the sake of all your kind.

'That you should exert your strength, without lagging or weariness.

'O Kandaka! * take this gem and going back to where my father is, take the jewel and lay it reverently before him, to signify my heart's relation to him.

'And then, for me, request the king to stifle every fickle feeling of affection, and say that I, to escape from birth and age and death, have entered on the wild (forest) of painful discipline.

'Not that I may get a heavenly birth, much less because I have no tenderness of heart, or that I cherish any cause of bitterness, but only that I may escape this weight of sorrow;

'The accumulated long-night weight of covetous desire, I now desire to ease the load (cause a break), so that it may be overthrown

* Kandaka was the charioteer of Buddha.

for ever, therefore I seek the way of ultimate escape;

'If I should obtain emancipation, then shall I never need to put away my kindred, to leave my home, to sever ties of love. "O! grieve not for your son." The five desires of sense beget the sorrow; those held by lust themselves induce the sorrow; my very ancestors, victorious kings have handed down to me their kingly wealth; I, thinking only on religion, put it all away; the royal mothers at the end of life leave their cherished treasures for their sons.

'Those sons who covet much such worldly profit: but I rejoice to have acquired religious wealth: if you say that I am young and tender, and that the time for seeking wisdom is not come, you ought to know that to seek true religion, there is never a time not fit; impermanence and fickleness, the hate of death, these ever follow us. And therefore I (embrace) the present day, convinced that now is time to seek religion.'

But by earnestness and diligence, then we conquer.

Walking in the path of true wisdom, letting go both extremes,* we then reach ultimate perfection.

Strength results alone from the mind's intention. 'If you remove (from conduct) the purpose of the mind, the bodily act is but as rotten wood; wherefore, regulate the mind, and then the body will spontaneously go right.

'What is reverenced, should be known and seen.

'Reverence indeed is due to righteous conduct, but let it not redound to the place (or, mode of life).

'My heart indeed is moved with affection towards you, for pleasant conversation is agreeable to all, those who listen are affected thereby.

'I know indeed that my royal father is possessed of a loving and deeply considerate mind, but my fear of birth, old age, disease

* The two extremes are worldly life and ascetic life.

and death have led me to disobey and disregard his extreme kindness.

'Whoever neglects right consideration about his present life, and because he hopes to escape in the end, therefore disregards all precautions (in the present) on this man comes the inevitable doom of death.

'It is the knowledge of this, therefore, that weighs with me, and after long delay has constrained me to a hermit's life; hearing of my father the king, and his grief, my heart is affected with increased love.

'But yet, all is like the fancy of a dream, quickly reverting to nothingness. Know then, without fear of contradiction, that the nature of existing things is not uniform.

'The cause of sorrow is not necessarily the relationship of child with parent, but that which produces the pain of separation, results from the influence of delusion;

'As men going along a road suddenly meet midway with others and then a moment more are separated, each one going his own way,

'So by the force of concomittance relationships are framed and then, according to each one's destiny, there is separation; he who thoroughly investigates this false connection of relationship ought not to cherish in himself grief;

'In this world there is rupture of family love, in another life (world) it is sought for again, brought together for a moment, again rudely divided, everywhere the fetters of kindred are formed!

'Ever being bound, and ever being loosened! who can sufficiently lament such constant separations; born into the world, and then gradually changing, constantly separated by death and then born again.

'All things which exist in time must perish, the forests and mountains all things thus exist; in time are born all sensuous things (things possessing the five desires), so is it both with worldly substance and with time.

'Because, then, death pervades all time, get rid of death, and time will disappear. You desire to make me king, and it is difficult to resist the offices of love;

'But as a disease (is difficult to bear) without medicine, so neither can I bear (this weight of dignity) ; in every condition, high or low, we find folly and ignorance, (and men) carelessly following the dictates of lustful passion ;

'At last, we come to live in constant fear : thinking anxiously of the outward form, the spirit droops ; following the ways of men, the mind resists the right ; but, the conduct of the wise is not so.

'The sumptuously ornamented and splendid palace (I look upon) as filled with fire ; the hundred dainty dishes (tastes) of the divine kitchen, as mingled with destructive poisons ;

'The lily growing on the tranquil lake in its midst harbors countless noisome insects ; and so the towering abode of the rich is the house of calamity ; the wise will not dwell therein.

'In former times illustrious kings, seeing the many crimes of their home and country, affecting as with poison the dwellers therein, in sorrowful disgust sought comfort in seclusion ;

'We know, therefore, that the troubles of a royal estate are not to be compared with the repose of a religious life ; far better dwell in the wild mountains, and eat the herbs like the beasts of the field;

'Therefore I dare not dwell in the wide palace, for the black snake has its dwelling there. I reject the kingly estate and the five desires (desires of the senses) to escape such sorrows I wander thro' the mountain wilds.

'This, then, would be the consequence of compliance, that I (who) delighting in religion, am gradually getting wisdom, should now quit these quiet woods, and returning home, partake of sensual pleasures,

'And thus by night and day increase my store of misery. Surely this is not what should be done! that the great leader of an illustrious tribe, having left his home from love of religion,

'And for ever turned his back upon tribal honour, desiring to confirm his purpose as a leader,—that he,—discarding outward form, clad in religious garb, loving religious meditation, wandering thro' the wilds,—

'Should now reject his hermit vestment, tread down his sense of proper shame (and give up his aim). This, tho' I gained heaven's kingly state, cannot be done! how much less to gain an earthly, though distinguished, home!

'For having spued forth lust, passion, and ignorance, shall I return to feed upon it? Such misery, how could I bear?

'Like a man whose house has caught fire, by some expedient finds a way to escape, will such a man forthwith go back and enter it again? such conduct would disgrace a man!

'So I, beholding the evils, birth, old age, and death, to escape the misery, have become a hermit; shall I then go back and enter in, and like a fool dwell in their company?

'He who enjoys a royal estate and yet seeks rescue, cannot dwell thus, this is no place for him; escape (rescue*) is born from quietness and rest;

'To seek for rest and yet aspire to royal condition is but a contradiction, royalty and rescue, motion and rest, like fire and water, having two principles, cannot be united.

'So one resolved to seek escape cannot

*Rescue here means rescue from sorrow or deliverance in the sense of salvation.

abide possessed of kingly dignity! and if you say a man may be a king, and at the same time prepare deliverance for himself,

'There is no certainty in this to seek certain escape is not to risk it thus; it is thro' this uncertain frame of mind that once a man gone forth is led to go back home again.

'But I, my mind is not uncertain; severing the baited hook of relationship with straightforward purpose, I have left my home. Then tell me, why should I return again?

'The question of being and not being is an idle one, only adding to the uncertainty of an unstable mind, and to talk of such matters I have no strong (fixed) inclination;

'Purity of life, wisdom, the practice of asceticism, these are matters to which I earnestly apply myself. The world is full of empty studies (discoveries) which our teachers in their office skilfully involve;

'But they are without any true principle, and I will none of them! The enlightened man distinguishes truth from falsehood; but how can truth * (faith) be born from such as those ?

'For they are like the man born blind, leading the blind man as a guide ; as in the night ; as in thick darkness (both wander on), what recovery is there for them ?

'Regarding the question of the pure and impure, the world involved in self-engendered doubt cannot perceive the truth ; better to walk along the way of purity,

'Or rather follow the pure law of self-denial, hate the practice of impurity, reflect on what was said of old, not obstinate in one belief or one tradition,

'With sincere (empty) mind, accepting all true words, and ever banishing sinful sorrow (*i.e.* sin, the cause of grief) words which exceed sincerity (simplicity of purpose) are vainly (falsely) spoken ; the wise man uses not such words.'

---

'Now, for your sakes, permit me briefly, to recount this one true principle (*i.e.*, purpose) (of action) :

* This word *truth* may also mean faith, according to the Chinese translation.

'"The sun, the moon may fall to earth, Sumeru and all the snowy mountains overturn, but I will never change my purpose; rather than enter a forbidden place,

'Let me be cast into the fierce fire; not to accomplish rightly (what I have entered on), and to return once more to my own land, there to enter the fire of the five desires,

'Let it befall me as my own oath records!"'

---

'In all the world, in its different sections, there is no chartered place for solid virtue (right principles),

'For if virtue flags and folly rules, what reverence can there be, or honour paid, to a high name or boast of prowess, inherited from former generations!

'And so there may be in the midst of great distress, large goodness, these are not mutually opposed. This then is so with the world in the connection of true worth and friendship.

'A true friend who makes good (free) use of wealth—is rightly called a fast and firm treasure, but he who guards and stints the profit he has made, his wealth will soon be spent and lost.

'The wealth of a country is no constant treasure, but that which is given in charity is rich in returns, therefore charity is a true friend, altho' it scatters, yet it brings no repentance;

'You indeed are known as liberal and kind. I make no reply in opposition to you but simply as we meet, so with agreeable purpose we talk.' *

These five desires, the inconstant thieves—stealing from men their choicest treasures, making them unreal, false, and fickle—are like the man called up as an apparition;

'For a time the beholders are affected (by it), but it has no lasting hold upon the mind; so these five desires are the great obstacles, for ever disarranging the way of peace;

'If the joys of heaven are not worth having, how much less the desires common to

---

* From Buddha's Reply to Bimbasara Raja.

men, begetting the thirst of wild love, and then lost in the enjoyment,

'As the fierce wind fans the fire, till the fuel be spent and the fire expires; of all unrighteous things in the world, there is nothing worse than the domain of the five desires;

'For all men maddened by the power of lust, giving themselves to pleasure, are dead to reason.

'The wise man fears these desires, he fears to fall into the way of unrighteousness;'

'Know then, that the province (indulgence) of the five desires is avowedly an enemy of the religious man.

'Covetousness and anger are as the serpent's poison.

'Like covering over with a false surface a hole full of fire, slipping thro' which, the body is burnt, so is the fire of covetous desire; the wise man meddles not with it.

'By coveting to appease these desires we really increase them, there is no character of permanency therefore about them.'

---

'Sorrow and joy cannot agree together, as a person slave-governed loses his renown.

'But religion causes all things to be of service, as a king reigning in his sovereignty; so religion controls sorrow, as one fits on a burthen according to power of endurance.

'Now then I pray you pity me not.

'Pity, rather, those who rule as kings!

'Their souls ever vacant and athirst, in the present world no repose, hereafter receiving pain as their meed.'

Second Edition, 2,000 Copies, July 1918. Natesan & Co., Madras.

# INDIAN POLITICAL LITERATURE

**Gandhi's Speeches and Writings.**—With an Introduction by Mr. Andrews and a biographical sketch of Gandhi by Mr. Polak. Cloth bound, indexed. Rs. 3. To Subscribers of "I.R." Rs. 2-8.

**Lord Sinha's Speeches & Writings.** With a biographical sketch & portrait. Rs. 3. To Subscribers of *I.R.* Rs. 2-8.

**Madan Mohan Malaviya's Speeches.** Cloth bound, Rs. 3. To Subscribers of "*I.R.*" Rs. 2-8.

**Gokhale's Speeches and Writings.**—Cloth bound. Third Edition. Price Rs. 4. To Subscribers of "I.R." Rs. 3-8.

**Surendranath Banerjea's Speeches and Writings.**—Comprehensive collection. Rs. 3. To Subscribers "I.R." Rs. 2-8.

**Wacha's Speeches and Writings.**—Comprehensive collection. Price Rs. 3. To Subscribers of "I.R." Rs. 2-8.

**Swami Vivekananda's Speeehes and Writings.**—Rs. 3. To Subscribers of "I.R." Rs. 2-8.

**Wedderburn's Speeches and Writings.**—An up-to-date collection. Price Rs. 3. To Subscribers of "I.R." Rs. 2-8.

**Dadabhai Naoroji's Speeches and Writings.**—Second Edition. Rs. 3. To Subscribers of "I. R." Rs. 2-8.

**Dr. P. C. Ray's Essays and Discourses.**—Rs. 3. To Subscribers of "I.R." Rs. 2-8.

**Sarojini Naidu's Speeches and Writings.** Second Edition. Price Re. 1-4. To Subscribers of "I.R." Re. 1.

**Montagu's Indian Speeches.**—A new and up-to-date edition. Price Re. 1-8. To Subscribers of "I.R." Re. 1-4.

**Morley's Indian Speeches.**—Crown 8vo., Revised and enlarged. Price Re. 1-8. To Subscribers of "I.R." Re. 1-4.

**Rash Behari Ghose's Speeches and Writings.** Second Edition. Re. 1-4. To Subscribers of "I.R." Re. One.

**King George's Speeches on Indian Affairs.** Price Re. One. To Subscribers of "I.R." As. 12.

**Mrs. Besant's Speeches and Writings on Indian Questions.** Price Re. 1-8. To Subscribers of "I.R." Re. 1-4.

☛ When ordering mention if you are a subscriber to the "Indian Review;" otherwise please note that concession rates will not be allowed. The annual subscription to the "Indian Review" is Rs. Five only. The price of a single copy is Re. One. Those who want books at concession rates must remit Rs. 5, one year's subscription in advance.

---

G. A. Natesan & Co., Sunkurama Chetty Street, Madras.

# HINDU RELIGION AND PHILOSOPHY

**Sri Sankaracharya.—I.—His Life and Times.** By C.N. Krishnaswamy Aiyar, M.A., L.T. II.—His Philosophy. By Pandit Sitanath Tattvabhushan. Both in one volume. As. 12. To Subscribers of "I.R." As. 8.

**Sri Madhwa and Madhwaism.**—A short Historic Sketch. By C. N. Krishnaswamy Aiyar, M.A. As. 12. To Subscribers of the "Indian Review," As. 8.

**Sri Ramanujacharya.**—His Life and Times. By S. Krishnaswami Aiyangar, M.A. His Philosophy. By T. Rajagopalachariar, M.A., B.L. As. 12. To Subscribers of the "Indian Review," As. 8.

**The Life and Teachings of Buddha.** By A. Dharmapala. Price As. 12. 2nd Edn. To Subscribers of "I. R.," As. 8.

**Sri Sankaracharya's Select Works.**—The Text in Sanskrit Devanagiri type and an English Translation. By S. Venkataramanan, B.A. Price Re. 1-8. To Subscribers of the "Indian Review," Re. 1.

**The Vaishnavaite Reformers of India.**—Critical Sketches of their Lives and Writings. By T. Rajagopalachariar, M.A., B.L. Price Re. 1. To Subscribers of "I.R." As. 12.

**Swami Vivekananda.**—An exhaustive and comprehensive collection of his speeches and writings. *With four portraits.* Fifth Edition. Price Rs. 3. To Subscribers of the "Indian Review," Rs. 2-8.

**Aspects of the Vedanta.** By various writers. Second Edition. As. 12. To Subscribers of the "I.R.," As. 8.

**Ten Tamil Saints.** By Mr. M. S. Purnalingam Pillai, B.A., L.T. Price As. 12. To Subscribers of "I.R.," As. 8.

**India's Untouchable Saints.** By K. V. Ramaswami, B.A., B.L. Price As. 6. To Subscribers of "I.R.," As. 4.

**Essentials of Hinduism.** As. 12. To Subscribers of "I.R.," As. 10.

**Hindu Psalms and Hymns.** By Mr. K. V. Ramaswami, B.A., B.L. Price As. 4.

**Maitreyi: A Vedic Story.** By Pandit Sitanath Tattvabhushan. Price As. 4.

**Vemana,** The Telugu Poet and Saint by Mr. C. Ramkrishna Rau. As. 4.

☞ *The Annual Subscription to the "REVIEW" is Rs. 5. (five). Subscription can commence from any month. Any one who wishes to buy books at the Concession rates must remit Rs. 5, (Five) one year's subscription to the "Indian Review" in advance.*

---

G.A. Natesan & Co., Publishers, George Town, Madras.